DON'T BE A FUCKING IDIOT
MAN'S ULTIMATE RELATIONSHIP GUIDE

BLAKE HILL

Bolt Press

Bolt Publishing
11150 W Olympic Blvd Suite 1000
Los Angeles, CA 90064

Copyright (C) 2025 by Blake Hill
ISBN-13: 978-0-982735-5-2
Library of Congress Control Number: 2025923761

Cover design: Dominic Forbes

All rights reserved.

First Bolt Publishing printing December 2025.
Visit byblakehill.com
Printed in the United States of America

Copyright © 2025 Blake Hill
All rights reserved.

For my younger self

CONTENTS

Foreword   7

Introduction   13

Chapter 1: Attachment Theory   19

Chapter 2: Love Languages   53

Chapter 3: Relationship Rituals   63

Conclusion   89

Bio   95

FOREWORD

Imagined and inspired by Dr. Ruth

When it comes to love, sex, and relationships, one thing is certain: nobody gets through life without a few bumps, bruises, and maybe even some spectacular wipeouts along the way. What matters is how you learn from them, laugh about them, and keep moving forward with a little more wisdom and, if you're lucky, a lot more connection.

This book you hold in your hands is not another dry, dusty psychological manual full of intimidating jargon. Oh no, this is something much better. It takes **Attachment Theory**, an idea from the brilliant John Bowlby in the 1950s, and breathes fresh life into it, with humor, relatable stories, and the kind of honesty most couples only whisper about behind closed doors.

I love the way the author explains the three main attachment styles, **secure, anxious, and avoidant**, all through playful animal metaphors. Secure people are like Golden Retrievers, wagging their tails and happy to cuddle. The anxious ones? Chihuahuas, barking for reassurance. And the avoidant partners? Well, they're cats, independent, aloof, and sometimes very difficult to coax out from under the bed. It's witty, yes, but it's also accurate. I've spent decades listening to couples, and let me tell you, sometimes you really do feel like you're trying to make a Chihuahua and a Cat live under the same roof.

But don't worry, this book is not here to scold you. Instead, it gently guides you toward understanding yourself and your partner, while sprinkling in laughter and stories that make you nod in recognition (and maybe blush a little). It shows you that **attachment styles aren't life sentences**, they're starting points. With self-awareness, therapy, and effort, anyone can grow toward a more secure, fulfilling style of love.

What really delights me about this work is that it doesn't stop at theory. It gives you **practical tools**: rituals for couples, tips for building trust, and reminders that love is both serious business and a grand comedy. Relationships are like tacos, motorcycles, or even sitcoms, you've got to enjoy the mess, not just the polished Instagram moments.

And let's not forget the discussion of **Love Languages**—physical touch, quality time, words of affirmation, acts of service, and receiving gifts. These aren't gimmicks; they're translations of the deepest desires of the heart. Combine that with an understanding of your attachment style, and you have a recipe for true intimacy.

The best part? This book is written with humor, humility, and lived experience. The author shares his own struggles with avoidance, his growth through self-awareness, and the ways meditation, surfing, and soul-searching helped him heal. That kind of honesty is a gift. It says, "See? You don't have to be perfect. You just have to keep showing up."

So, my dear readers, buckle up. Or better yet, kick off your shoes, sit on the beach, and let these pages make you laugh, reflect, and maybe even change the way you see yourself and your partner.

Because love isn't just a theory. It's a practice. A daily ritual. A choice. And if you're willing to do the work, whether you're a Retriever, a Chihuahua, or a Cat, you can build the kind of connection that doesn't just last, but thrives.

As I always say: **Don't just talk about love, make love. And never stop learning about it.**

— Blake Hill
Author, imagining the spirit of Dr. Ruth

INTRODUCTION

INTRODUCTION

Why did I write this book? Because I got goddamn tired of watching good men burn down the house and I've done my fair share of lighting the match as well. Sixty years on this spinning rock, and I've loved deep, crashed harder and had the universe slap me across the face more times than I can count. I was married for twenty years before being handed divorce papers that hit like a sledgehammer to the soul. My last book, *Westfalia*, was born out of that wreckage. I thought I was writing about heartbreak, loss and divorce, but what poured out was a spiritual exorcism on two wheels. I wasn't just driving away from a broken marriage. I was driving straight into the abyss of my soul.

My mind became a confession booth, my altar, and my punching bag. Every mile I rode stripped away another layer of bullshit, my pride, my resentment, my illusions of control. *Westfalia* was a pilgrimage of sorts, fueled by heartbreak, black coffee, and raw honesty. It was where I met my younger self, the kid who learned early how to survive but not how to love. And when that kid showed up, so did my demons. I didn't fight them this time. I sat with them, listened, and sometimes cursed at them between stops.

I devoured books like *Attachment Theory* and *Love Languages* the way some guys devour whiskey, hoping they'd numb the ache or at least explain it. I wanted to understand why I craved love yet feared it, why I kept replaying the same damn patterns expecting a different ending. I dug deep, even when it got ugly. There I was. outside on a bicycle, hauling my pain across Canada. Ten thousand feet of elevation, one hundred and ten miles a day, lungs burning, spirit breaking open. Somewhere between exhaustion and awakening, a bear charged me, I understood something simple, ego will get you killed, in the wild and in love. Stay calm.

This book isn't about becoming enlightened or perfect. It's about getting your shit together enough to show up as a man worth loving. It's about killing the ego that keeps you defensive and quieting the fear that keeps you small. It's for men who still believe in raw, honest connection, but are done pretending they've got it all figured out.

If *Westfalia* was the story of my resurrection, *Don't Be a Fucking Idiot* is the gospel according to the scars, the manual I wish I had before I burned down the house of love. It's gritty, it's spiritual, it's honest as fuck. So crack open a beer, drop the armor, and let's talk man to man.

CHAPTER ONE

ATTACHMENT THEORY

While attachment theory may sound like a dry, boring, and academic topic, it actually has a lot to say about the ups and downs of relationships. So, let's dive into a lighthearted look at Adult Attachment Theory and how it affects our lives and romantic relationships. Let's dive deeper into each attachment style. Are you anxious, avoidant, fearful-avoidant or secure? What is your wife, girlfriend, partner, baby momma?

Attachment Styles
Love, Leashes, and Rough Seas

Love isn't a calm harbor, it's a goddamn ocean. One minute you're floating under pink skies, hand on the wheel, everything steady and fine. The next, you're in a squall, waves slamming, heart pounding, and you're wondering if this thing you built can even stay afloat. Do you panic? Are you calm? Do you run? Attachment styles are how we sail it. They're the map, the compass, the muscle memory in your hands when the sky goes dark. They're also the dogs and cats inside us, loyal or wild, grounded or skittish, ready to love or ready to bolt.

Psychologists John Bowlby and Mary Ainsworth first charted these waters, tracing how our earliest experiences shape the way we reach for, or run from love. Later, Mary Main, Phillip Shaver, and Cindy Hazan took the theory into adulthood, proving that the same emotional weather that formed us as kids still storms inside us as grown-ups.

So meet the four sailors in your soul, the Retriever, the Chihuahua, the Cat, and the Feral, each trying to navigate the same unpredictable sea called relationships.

Secure Attachment
Golden Retriever at the Helm

If you're Securely Attached, you're the Golden Retriever of the seas, loyal, calm, a steady captain who doesn't lose their shit when the clouds roll in. You grew up in a harbor that held steady, love that showed up, consistency that taught your nervous system that storms pass, and the ship still floats.

You don't need to chase, panic, or hide below deck. You trust the process, trust yourself, and trust that love doesn't vanish when it gets quiet. You know when to furl the sails, when to let the wind carry you, and when to drop anchor and rest.

Being with you feels like balance, a steady deck under bare feet even when the waves hit. You don't confuse calm with boredom or space with rejection. You know love's supposed to breathe.

You're not immune to pain, but you don't let fear steer the boat. You can argue without detonating, forgive without forgetting, and stay when the easy option would be to drift away.

That's not luck, that's skill. It's what happens when someone learned early that connection doesn't have to hurt.

Anxious Attachment
The Chihuahua in the Tempest

Then there's the Anxious type. The annoying Chihuahua with a sailor's soul, shaking in the storm, yapping at the thunder, and scanning the horizon for signs of love drifting away.

You grew up in unpredictable weather, affection one day, silence the next. You learned to survive by staying alert, reading every gust of emotional wind: Are they okay? Are they pulling away? Am I losing them?

So now, in adulthood, you clutch the wheel too tight. You check your texts like a rat on crack looking for cheese. You think if you just hold on harder, you can stop the storm from coming. You crave closeness so badly that sometimes you start swimming even when the boat's still afloat.

You love deep and hard, maybe too hard for people who've never had to fight for it. You give everything, then blame yourself when it's not enough. But your sensitivity isn't weakness, it's sonar. You just need to learn to trust your reading of the tides, waves, and wind.

Calm water isn't danger. Silence isn't abandonment. It's peace, something you were never taught to recognize.

Once you do, you become one of the most powerful lovers out there: loyal, intuitive, and emotionally fearless.

Stop apologizing for your depth. The ocean needs people who feel it all.

Avoidant Attachment
The Cool Cat Adrift

Avoidants are the Cats of the relationship world, sleek, self-sufficient, and allergic to emotional leashes. You're the lone sailor who swears you don't need a crew. Freedom is your oxygen, and vulnerability feels like a storm you never signed up for.

You grew up with cold winds, love that was distant, unpredictable, or conditional. You learned early: Don't rely on anyone. So you built your own damn ship. You charted solo routes. You got so good at steering alone that now, even when someone wants to join you, it feels like a threat.

You crave closeness but fear losing control. You want the warmth, but when someone reaches for you, your sails tighten, and before you know it, you're halfway to open water again.

You call it independence, but sometimes it's just loneliness in disguise.

You're not broken, you're guarded. You've been burned by waves before, so you keep your distance. But the truth is, the boat's sturdier than you think.

Let someone tie up alongside you for once. You can still roam, still chart your own course, just with a second heartbeat on deck. Love doesn't have to steal your freedom; it can make the voyage worth taking.

Disorganized / Fearful-Avoidant
Feral Cat in the Hurricane

And then there's the Disorganized, the Fearful-Avoidant. The feral cat on a ship in a hurricane. Half wild, half desperate, full of love and lightning.

This is the style Mary Main, Phillip Shaver, and Cindy Hazan identified as the paradox, the sailor steering straight into the storm, praying for rescue but flinching at every touch.

You grew up in chaos, where the person meant to keep you safe was also the source of your fear. You learned to crave comfort and brace for pain at the same time. The result? A compass that never stops spinning.

You reach for love, then panic when it gets close. You pour your heart out one night and disappear the next. You test, you pull, you push, not because you want drama but because you're terrified of calm. Calm feels foreign. Calm feels like the silence before something breaks.

But inside that storm lives the most profound kind of heart, one that knows the cost of love and still dares to want it.

Once you start to separate the old weather from the new, once you realize this sky isn't the same one that hurt you, everything changes.

You become the survivor who can read the wind better than anyone. You stop running from the waves and start steering through them. You become the captain of your own chaos. You are fierce, awake, and unstoppable.

You're not too much. You're just a heart that's been through hell and still beats with hope. That's not broken, that's brave.

Final Thoughts
Love's Weather Report

Every one of us carries a little fur and a little saltwater. We're all some mix of instinct and fear, leash and sail. Some of us chase. Some of us hide. Some of us anchor down and hold steady no matter what.

Your attachment style isn't a flaw, it's your chart. It's not your fate, it's your navigational tool. You can re-learn the stars. You can patch the sails. You can decide that the next time the wind howls, you won't abandon ship.

Because love isn't the absence of storms. It's two people standing soaked to the bone, gripping the ropes, yelling over the chaos, *"Alright, we've got this. Let's ride it out together."*

I have come to realize that I tend to display avoidant attachment style behavior in my relationships. This can make it difficult for me to form deep, meaningful connections with others, and has often left me feeling alone and disconnected. Despite this, I have been dedicated to my inner journey, and have invested a significant amount of time and effort into my own emotional growth.

My journey in cultivating a more secure attachment style has been a challenging one, and I have encountered many obstacles along the way. Although

I have done an enormous amount of inner emotional work on myself, I still find that I revert to avoidant style behaviors when my stress and anxiety levels are high. During these moments, I have found that engaging in activities such as meditation, surfing, hiking, and bike riding can help me reduce my stress levels and promote a greater sense of inner peace. Let's take surfing for example. Plunging myself into the ocean is enough to reset my inner dialog and create a sense that all is well in my world. But if I'm able to catch a few waves, that's icing on the cake. My life will feel complete. The other day I sat alone on the peak and had a full blown conversation with myself. Yes. Out-loud. I ask myself questions and in the end my final advice was. "Wake up motherfucker and get busy fixing the situation." Find what works for you, and do it.

Through extensive soul searching, I have come to a greater understanding of my attachment style and how it has impacted my relationships. It has taken me a fair amount of time to come to this realization, but I am grateful for the insights that I have gained. By acknowledging my tendencies towards avoidance and developing healthy coping skills, I am taking an active step towards building more secure and fulfilling relationships with my life-partner.

While the journey towards cultivating a more secure attachment style can be challenging, I remain committed to this process of emotional growth and self- awareness. I believe that by continuing to work on myself and staying focused on my personal development goals, I can overcome these challenges and build healthier, more fulfilling connections with my relationship.

Here are some light-hearted stories of various attachment styles in relationships of friends that I have observed over the years..

Secure dating an Anxious

There was a secure attachment friend named Tom, who fell in love with Sara. Tom's demeanor would be considered a classic Golden Retriever. He is friendly, warm, and always ready to nuzzle up on the couch and watch a movie or even fetch a frisbee. Sara on the other hand, was more like a Chihuahua, always yapping for attention and worrying about everything. In the beginning of the relationship Tom thought Sara's nervous energy was sweet and kind of cute. He would stroke her back and tell her everything was going to be okay and she would curl up next to him and feel a little better. But as the relationship went on, Tom began to feel like he was walking on eggshells. Sara would get upset if he didn't text back right away, or comment on her instagram posts or if he wanted to spend time with his friends instead of just the two of them.

One day, Tom came home from work to find Sara pacing back and forth in the living room, her voice quivering and her energy riddled with anxiety. "What's wrong?" Tom asked, trying to stay calm and centered. Sara said, "I… I just feel like you don't really love me." As she paced back and forth in the room.

Tom felt his heart sink, "Of course I love you, Sara. You know that." Sara shook her head no and said, "But how do I know for sure? What if you meet someone else and leave me?"

Tom drew in a deep breath of compassion mixed with empathy. He knew Sara's anxiety was not her fault and that he needed to be patient and understanding with her. He said, "listen Sara. I'm not going anywhere. I love you and I want to be with you. But I also need you to trust me and believe in our relationship. Can we work on that together?"

Sara's anxiety shifted to embarrassment as her eyes filled with tears. "I'm sorry, Tom. I know I'm being ridiculous. I just can't help it sometimes. I want too but I just can't. I'm sorry." Tom wrapped his arms around her and pulled her close. He said, "It's okay, Sara. I got you. We'll work on it together. And hey, if you ever need a break from all the worrying, I know a great dog park where we can play fetch!" Sara couldn't help but laugh and for a moment, the anxiety melted away like snow on a warm spring day. Tom's reassurance and secure attachment behavior gave Sara the feeling that everything was going to be okay after all.

Are you Tom or are you Sara within your relationship? At the end of the day we all have a lot to learn about ourselves and our significant other and how we can apply the knowledge we have gained to create a more thriving relationship.

Secure with an Avoidant

Lisa is a secure attachment person who fell in love with an avoidant named Mike. Lisa was the Golden Retriever in this story. She was warm, friendly and always ready to cuddle up with Mike. He, on the other hand, was more like an alley cat, independent, aloof, and sometimes very hard to read.

At first Lisa was attracted to Mike's independence. She enjoyed having her own space and she respected Mike's need for autonomy. But as the relationship went, she started to feel she was receiving mixed signals. Mike would seem interested one minute and then disappear into his man-cave the next. He was guarded with his emotions and rarely talked about his feelings. Lisa was unsure how to get him to open up.

One night Lisa decided to surprise Mike with a romantic dinner at home. She cooked his favorite meal, lit some candles and jazz music filled the room. When mike walked in the door, Lisa met him wearing a black skinny dress with tall high heel shoes and a mischievous, seductive smile. She reached for his hand and said, "hey there, good looking." She pulled him in tight and wrapped her arms around his shoulders and pressed her breast into him. Mike looked startled, like he had just seen a ghost. He stumbled with his words as he said, "Huh, hey Lisa. What's all this?" Lisa smiled with seduction and said, "I thought we could have a nice, intimate dinner together. Are you game?"

Mike hesitated, "I don't know, Lisa. I'm not really in the mood. I just don't feel it tonight."

Lisa's heart sank with disappointment. She had been hoping for a romantic evening and now it seemed like mike wasn't interested. But then she had an idea. She took a deep breath and maintained her composure.

She stepped back and looked him in the eyes and said, "okay, I get it. No problem." Reaching into her purse. "I have a plan B." Lisa pulled out a red laser pointer and aimed it at the wall. Suddenly, a red dot appeared and Mike's eyes latched onto it. His body puffed up with excitement as he said, "ohh, a laser pointer!" Lisa grinned, "yep! It's my secret weapon. Now come on, let's play!"

Lisa and Mike spent the rest of the evening chasing the little red dot around the room, like a couple of cats playing with a toy. It wasn't the romantic evening Lisa had planned, but it was still a lot of fun. Maybe Mike was an avoidant, but he was also kind of adorable in a cat like way to her.

As they snuggled up on the couch, Lisa felt a sense of contentment wash over her. Without trying to change Mike's attachment style, she found a way to connect with him and enjoy their time together. And who knows, maybe next time he'll purr like a contented cat in her lap.

Avoidant with Anxious

Max was an avoidant attachment person who started dating Dolly who was anxious. Max was like a fox, intelligent, independent, aloof, and really hard to read. Dolly on the other hand was like a Pomeranian, always yapping for attention and constantly worrying about everything with nervous energy.

In the beginning Max found Dolly's anxious energy amusing. He would roll his eyes at her constant fretting, but secretly he liked how much she seemed to care about him. Dolly though was always on edge, worried that Max was going to leave her at any time and for any reason.

One morning, Dolly called Max in a panic. This event had happened many times. Max let out a big sigh as he listened to her. She said, "Max! I had a really bad nightmare last night. It was so bad. You left me for your ex-wife!"

Max rolled his eyes and let out a big sigh. He was emotionally drained and growing extremely tired of having to constantly reassure her. Max said, "Dolly, it was just a dream. I'm not going anywhere." But Dolly wouldn't let it go. She said with utter nervousness, "But what if it's not just a dream, Max? What if you really do leave me?"

Max felt consumed with frustration as his tone became sharp. He said, "Dolly, I'm not going anywhere, I'm not going to leave you. I love you. Okay? But you need to calm down!"

Dolly stood there with tears rolling down her cheeks. She said, "I can't help it, Max. I love you so much and I can't imagine living without you. I don't want to lose you!"

Max felt guilty for making her cry but he was also extremely frustrated with her. He didn't know how to handle her constant need for reassurance and incessant insecurities." Her anxious energy and constant emotional need had drained his energy. One piece of him wanted to shut down and put an end to the relationship. And in that moment he was flooded with an idea.

He said, "Ok Dolly. I'll make you a deal. I'll promise to stay with you for a year and if we're still happy together after that year. We'll renew our verbal contract for each other. And then we'll see how we feel after that. Does that work for you?"

Dolly was semi-skeptical, but also intrigued. She said, "Ok, Max. Let's do it." So, Max drew up a contract, complete with legalese and fine print.

They both signed it and for the next year. They were officially a couple. Whenever Dolly became flooded with anxiousness, Max would point to the contract and remind her that they had a whole year together.

To everyone's surprise, the contract actually worked. Dolly felt more secure, knowing that Max was committed to her for a set period of time and Max felt less pressure by her constant need for reassurance. They started to have fun with it, joking about the "terms and conditions" of their relationship.

In the end, they renewed the contract for another year, and then another. Even though it felt a little weird, they both knew that they had found a way to make their relationship work. Max is an avoidant and Dolly is anxious, but together they created a space where a Fox and a Pomeranian could live a life together.

Avoidant with a Fearful-Avoidant

It's a rare occasion that an Avoidant would attract an Avoidant but let's write a story and see what happens.

There were two avoidant attachment people named Jack and Diane, who were engaged to be married. Jack was the Fearful-Avoidant - always keeping his emotions in check, never allowing himself to get too attached and preferring to spend most of his time alone, he didn't need anyone. Diane was similar - she valued her false independence and didn't like to feel tied down by anyone or anything.

At first, it seemed like the perfect relationship. They could both go days without talking to each other and neither one of them seemed to mind. They would make plans to hang out, but then cancel at the last minute and neither one was bothered by it. They were both content in their bubble of avoidance.

But then, things started to get a little weird. One day, Jack called Diane in a panic, "Jill, I have a problem. I really need someone to talk to." Diane was taken aback and asked, "What's wrong Jack? Are you okay?"

"I don't know." Jack said, sounding genuinely distressed. "I feel like I'm losing my sense of detachment. I keep thinking about you all the time and I can't seem to shake this feeling that I need you in my life. I don't want to go through this false motion of an engagement, I want to live it and feel it."

Diane was shocked. She had never heard Jack so emotional before. She said with hesitation, "Uh okay, Jack. That's... good, I guess?"

Jack wasn't done and said, "Diane, I keep having these weird dreams where we're married and have kids and live in a two-story house with a white picket fence but I die!"

This is really worrisome for Diane and makes her feel uncomfortable. She says, "Jack, are you sure you're okay? Maybe you should see a therapist?" Jack laughed, "No way, Diane. I'm not that far gone. I just need to get my avoidance back under control." And with that, he hung up.

Diane didn't know what to do. She was an avoidant too, but even she couldn't deny the weirdness of Jack's sudden emotional outburst.

The days turned into weeks and Diane didn't hear from Jack. She tried to reach out to him, but he didn't respond. She began to wonder if he had gone completely off the rails. And then out of nowhere, he called her. "Diane, I've got it under control now. I went on a solo camping trip and did some deep soul searching. I know I can be avoidant again now."

Diane was relieved, but also a little annoyed. She said, "Jack, what are we doing here? If we're both avoidant, how are we supposed to have a relationship?"

Jack laughed, "Well Diane, maybe we don't need a traditional relationship, perhaps we need a non-relationship. Like NSA, No-Strings-Attached or FWP, Friends With Privileges. We'll avoidant date instead of being engaged.

Diane shook her head with doubt and said, "That's the stupidest thing you've ever said, Jack. But it does kinda make sense. They both like their independence and they both valued their space. Maybe it was possible to have a relationship defined by their emotional needs without all the societal baggage.

So, Jack and Diane continued their avoidant "dating," never putting a label on what they were to each other, but very content in their mutual avoidance attachment. It might not have been a fairy tale romance, but it worked for them and who knows, maybe one day they will both work through their avoidant attachment and actually allow themselves to fall in love. For now, they are content being two avoidant ships passing through the night.

Anxious with Anxious

The perfect Anxious storm collided when Paula and Trent began dating. Paula was a nervous wreck most of the time, always worrying about what could go wrong in any given situation. Trent was always anxious about making the right impression and saying the right things.

Their first date was a complete disaster. Paula spent the entire time worrying about what Trent thought about her and whether or not he was having a good time. Trent, meanwhile was so nervous that he spilled his red wine all over his white button-down shirt and spent the rest of the night feeling embarrassed and self-conscious.

Although they had such a rocky start, they didn't give up and decided to give it another try, and another, and another. Each date was filled with awkward silence, nervous laughter, and a constant fretting about every little detail.

One sunny day, Trent decided to surprise Paula with a romantic picnic in the park. He spent hours carefully packing the perfect meal and setting up a cozy blanket in the shade under a tree. When Paula arrived, she was thrilled but as they sat down to eat, her attention was caught by a bee buzzing around.

"Trent, do you see that bee?" She asked with a tremble in her voice. "What if it stings us? What if I have an allergic reaction? What if I need to go to the hospital?"

Trent felt the picnic was a disaster and it was all his fault. He had put so much effort into making this the perfect date and now it was being ruined from a bee that he didn't think to check for. The bee buzzed both of them as they both stood up and ran. Trent tripped over a hidden log in the grass and as he laid there pondering the situation. He had a moment of clarity, realizing they're both so anxious and decided to try something new, a different approach. He stood up and decided to make a simple decision that seemed so huge for him.

"Paula." He called out, "It's okay. We can handle a bee. Let's just ignore it and eat our food while enjoying each other and we'll deal with what comes up."

Paula was hesitant and skeptical as she drew in a deep breath and tried to relax. To her surprise, the bee flew away. They were able to enjoy the rest of their picnic without any further incidents, not even a wine spill.

As they were packing up, Paula turned to Trent and said, "You know, Trent, I never thought I would find someone who was a anxious as I am. It's really comforting to know that I'm not alone in all of this.

Trent smiled, "Yeah Paula, me too. I think we can help each other through our anxiety and learn to enjoy life a little more."

They both felt a weight lift from their shoulders. Although they may never be the most care-free couple, they were happy in their own anxious way. Who knows, maybe someday they will be able to face the unknown side of life without freaking out. For now, they were happy to have found each other.

Secure with Secure

When two secure attachments collide, is it a fairy-tale ending? Meet John and Emma, they have been together for three years. Each of them is a well-adjusted, confident individual who doesn't carry a lot of baggage or possess hang-ups. They are totally happy-go-lucky people who enjoy one another.

Their first date was simple and easy. They went to a casual restaurant and had a nice dinner, chatting and laughing the whole time. They both felt very comfortable around each other right away and their conversation flowed without having to struggle to connect.

As they continued to date, they found that they had a lot in common. Both loved hiking, working out, reading spiritual books and watching funny movies. One of their favorite things to do was trying new restaurants and exploring the city. Both were focused on their careers and didn't feel any pressure to rush into anything super serious with their relationship. They wanted to let it unfold naturally.

One day, John decided to take Emma on a surprise adventure. He blindfolded her and led her to his car, promising it would all be worth it. Emma was naturally a little apprehensive but excited about the surprise element. She trusted John and sat in the front seat with giddiness.

After a short drive, they arrived at a small airport. John took off her blindfold and revealed that they were going on a hot air balloon ride. Emma was amazed and super excited to ride in the balloon. They climbed into the basket and floated into the clear blue sky while enjoying breathtaking views and the cool crisp morning air all while holding hands.

As they floated along in the quietness of the morning with the occasional burst of sound from the thruster. John turned to Emma and said, "You know Emma, I feel like we're both pretty secure in who we are and what we want. We don't allow a lot of drama or chaos in our lives. We're happy being ourselves and being together."

Emma smiled in agreement and said, "I know, John. It's such a relief to be with someone who doesn't have a lot of baggage or hang-ups. We can enjoy each others company and have fun with life." They embraced in the golden morning light and consumed the beauty before them as they continued to float along, happy and secure in their own little bubble. They might not of had the most exciting or dramatic relationship but they were happy in their own simple, secure way.

Of course these are a few examples of stories that illustrate challenges and rewards that different attachment styles can bring to a relationship and thus help you to define what attachment style you most identify with. Once you allow yourself to have a greater awareness of yourself and your wife's needs, you'll better understand how to support the relationship.

It's best to understand that our attachment style is not set in concrete. With self- awareness and effort, it's possible to develop a more secure attachment style and build a healthier, more satisfying relationship. So, whether you're a Golden Retriever, Cat, Fox, Chihuahua, or Pomeranian. Remember, love and connection lie within our reach, providing an ever-present guiding light of hope.

I'd like to thank and give credit to John Bowlby, a British Psychoanalyst, who in the 1950s developed The Attachment Theory Framework that explains how early childhood experiences shape our ability to form and maintain close relationships throughout our lives. According to Mr. Bowlby, children develop an attachment style based on their interactions with their primary caregivers, usually their mother and/or father. These interactions shape the child's expectations about whether or not they can rely on others to meet their needs.

Overall, attachment theory helps to explain why some people have more successful relationships than others and provides insight into how individuals can work to improve their relationships by understanding their own attachment style and that of their partner.

This is a golden opportunity to interrupt the destructive pattern of toxic relationships and educate future generations on how to foster healthy and loving connections.

Now that you can identify your attachment style and that of your wife, girlfriend, you have to ask yourself; how do I proceed and what do I want to gain? I personally used the knowledge of the attachment styles to find a greater understanding of myself. And my philosophy has always been, you need to fulfill your own needs and not expect others to fulfill those for you. This is why it's so important to fully understand why someone is the way they are. There's a balance that comes into play here with how we use our attachment style. It doesn't excuse bad behavior nor should it be used to manipulate your partner. Once you have identified with your attachment style, now it's time to go to work on yourself and dig deep with a therapist. If your car had a flat, would you continue driving on a flat tire or would you fix it? Going to a therapist is a good thing. It's a place where we can gain the tools to elevate a better emotional life for ourselves. The goal of anyone who does not come from a secure attachment style, is to implement the secure style within your life so that you can live a healthier, happier life with yourself and that chick who sleeps beside you. One last note, not all relationships last forever.

CHAPTER TWO

LOVE LANGUAGES

The idea of Love Languages was first introduced by Dr. Gary Chapman in his book, "The Five Love Languages: How To Express Heartfelt Commitment to Your Mate." According to Dr Chapman, there are five main love languages that people use to give and receive love. These love languages are: Physical Touch, Quality Time, Words Of Affirmation, Acts Of Service, and Receiving Gifts.

Love is a complex and complicated emotion that holds immense power and importance in our lives. I perceive God as the embodiment of Love reflecting a spiritual understanding of the profound nature of this emotion. When I describe

God as Love, I detach the concept from any specific religious or spiritual belief system and instead focus on the core principle that love is a universal force. By acknowledging this divine force, I recognize that love has the potential to be the foundation for every aspect of our lives. Viewing love as the underlying energy that permeates our existence allows us to tap into its infinite source. When we tap into this source of love, we can undergo personal transformation and bring about positive change in the world around us, including our relationships with our partners. Living from a place of love involves cultivating acts of kindness, empathy, and understanding towards others. It requires deep personal connection and a genuine desire to bring about harmony and well-being. By embracing love as the guiding principle in our lives, we can foster strong and nurturing relationships with our significant other. Living from love means approaching our interactions with kindness, compassion, and a willingness to understand and support our loved ones. It involves being present, actively listening, and engaging in acts of service that demonstrate our love and care. It also entails acknowledging and accepting our own imperfections and those of our partners, nurturing forgiveness and growth. Living from love doesn't mean that challenges or discord won't arise. However, it provides us with the capacity to approach them with grace, understanding, and a commitment to finding resolutions that honor the well-being and happiness of both individuals. Ultimately, living from love is a powerful choice that can profoundly impact our lives and the lives of those around us. By embracing love as the leading force in our relationships, we can create deeper connections, promote understanding, and contribute to a more balanced and compassionate world.

PHYSICAL TOUCH

People who have a physical touch love language, feel loved when they receive physical touch from their partner. This can include things like holding hands, hugging, kissing, gentle playful touches while passing one another, and spooning before going to sleep. Physical touch is the foremost way of expressing love for these type of individuals. Maybe consider taking a massage class together. Don't go straight for the goal, allow the energy to build.

QUALITY TIME

Those who have a Quality Time love language feel loved when they spend quality time with their partner. This means giving you partner your undivided attention and participating in activities together that you both enjoy. And no, that doesn't mean that your wife drives the golf cart while you play eighteen or sits on the beach filming you while you catch waves. Set time aside to do an activity you both enjoy. If you're going out to dinner, leave your phone in the car or if you have to carry it, don't put it on the table.

WORDS OF AFFIRMATION

People who have a Words Of Affirmation love language feel loved when they receive verbal affirmations from their partner. This can include compliments, words of encouragement, expressing gratitude, and saying I love you. Be real, most women want to hear you say what you feel. Don't just say the same thing over and over. Be creative with your compliments, dig deep and give her some juicy nuggets that light up her emotions.

ACTS OF SERVICE

People who have an Acts Of Service love language feel loved when their partner does things for them. This can include cooking dinner, doing the laundry, serving breakfast in bed, foot rub (physical touch) wash their car, put the kids to bed, night at a hotel, flowers. Keep it simple and make it frequent. Remember actions speak louder than words. When you do something for her, don't rush to proclaim you did it, you're not a two-year-old. Let her be surprised.

RECEIVING GIFTS

Who doesn't like to receive gifts? People who have a receiving gifts love language feel loved when they receive gifts from their partner. These gifts don't have to be expensive, but they should be thoughtful and meaningful. Are you listening? Because that's what it's going to take for you to understand what your significant other might want as a gift. Make it a thoughtful and sentimental gift. Did they ask you for a gift or give you a list? Are you celebrating a special occasion? If so, perhaps a themed gift with a unique flair would make that special occasion ultra amazing. This is a great time to use AI, to find an amazing and unique gift based on your budget.

Do you understand your Love Language? It's important to understand yourself in the same way you have to love yourself before you can love someone else. So take some time to think and reflect on the different ways in which you feel loved. Do you feel loved when your wife gives you a gift or is it physical touch? You can take a test online to find your love language. And then have your partner take the test. Once you have identified your own love language communicate this to your partner so they have a better understanding of how to show you love. Understanding your wife's love language can sometimes feel like trying to decode an ancient language. But it doesn't have to be so serious. Remember to communicate with you partner, be open to change. One common misconception about love languages is that they are set in concrete and will not change. It's important to know that love languages can change as we grow, evolve, and mature as individuals and within our relationships. Do your best to make an effort to express your love in a manner that exemplifies to her how much you care for her.

CHAPTER THREE

RELATIONSHIP RITUALS

Enduring relationships entail a journey of life's ups and downs, requiring commitment, perseverance, compassion, empathy, affection, love, and respect from two people. One of the keys to a successful and fulfilling marriage is the development of positive-emotional-and-physical rituals.

Enduring relationships, those that somehow survive the test of time and the maddening jigsaw puzzle of life, are like an epic adventure. Think Indiana Jones, but with less running from boulders and more running from arguments about who forgot to take out the trash. Relationships are like a tasty taco, made up of layers of commitment (the tortilla that holds everything together), perseverance (the cheese that adds flavor), compassion (the lettuce that adds a crunch), empathy (the greasiness that smooths everything out), affection (the tomatoes that add a refreshing bite), love (the meat of the matter), and respect (the hot sauce that gives it zing).

Now, if you're thinking of a successful and fulfilling marriage, think of it as a workout routine. You've got to develop some positive, emotional and physical habits, much like those you'd expect to run a marathon, go surfing or lift weights, but with less exhaustion and more understanding. This means enhancing an environment where you can express your feelings without judgement, kind of like how you'd want to cry out when you stub your toe on the coffee table, but with less cursing.

The physical side of things is just as important. No, I'm not talking about bench pressing your partner, but maintaining intimacy over time. It's like doing the Cha-Cha-Cha, with less tripping over your feet and more tottering over the charming, small, everyday acts of affection. It's about creating a rhythm of togetherness, like cooking together, except you try not to burn the house down.

At the end of the day, think of an enduring relationship like a sitcom. There's laughter, tears, challenges, plot twists, and commercial breaks. It's a journey of two people, with their own scripts, quirks, and dumb jokes, trying to make their way through life, hoping each season is better than the last. So, sit-back, buckle up, and enjoy the ride, and let yourself laugh along the way.

Instead of using the word habit, I have placed ritual in its place. A ritual seems more symbolic for a positive outcome versus a habit which has a negative context in my opinion.

Rituals, in their simplest form, are actions or behaviors that we've repeated so often that they've become bored and decided to move into our brain permanently. They're like that one catchy song that gets stuck in your head, repeating itself until you can't think of anything else, except instead of singing "Baby Shark" on repeat, you're flossing your teeth or going for a dawn-patrol surf.

Rituals can be as simple as brushing your teeth every morning or as complex as driving a car, which if you think about it, is essentially just playing a real-life video game without the luxury of rebooting. Once a habit is established, it's like your brain goes on autopilot, making you do these things without so much as a second thought.

Rituals are basically the ring leader of our lives. They're like that planner-phenom-friend who plans everything to the T. Eating healthily, working out, biting your nails, or even binge-watching an entire season of Yellowstone in one night, all these things are habits (rituals) calling the shots from the shadows of our sub-conscious.

The science peeps tell us it takes about 66 days to form a new habit, but let's be real, that's just an average. It could take you two weeks to start drinking more water or two years to stop yourself from eating that entire quart of ice cream or box of thin mint cookies in one sitting (yes! I do it too!). When it comes to relationships, rituals are like the script of an ongoing Netflix series. They decide whether the show is a delightful comedy, dark comedy or a tragic drama. But hey, the good news is that we can always rewrite the script, one ritual at a time.

It may take a while, it might be like teaching a dog to meow, but with a little perseverance and a lot of reruns, it's absolutely possible. Remember, houses aren't built in a day, nor award-winning shows. Healthy rituals take time.

Breaking a habit can be influenced by various factors, such as the complexity, how frequently you engage in the behavior, and your level of commitment to breaking the habit. Think of it like that enthusiastic roommate who's decided to learn the electric guitar at 2 am. Sometimes it's annoyingly unique, but most times it's way off beat. The complexity of the habit, its frequency, and your commitment to changing the tune all play a role in this.

It's like that person who forgets to replace the toilet paper roll, a little annoying, but usually, a gentle reminder does the trick. Now, obsessively checking social media? That's like being with someone who's taken up beatboxing at dawn. It requires a tad more patience and possibly a good headset.

Keep in mind, some habits are like that quart of mint chocolate chip ice cream you scarf down at midnight, they're there to help you cope when you're stressed or anxious. But just as you wouldn't eat ice cream for every meal, relying on one habit too much can make your life chaotic.

Breaking a habit can feel like trying to surf for the first time, it's challenging, you're off balance, and there's an extremely good chance you'll fall off a few times. But strategies like figuring out what causes you to fall (your triggers), or replacing the habit with something more constructive (like practicing yoga instead of trying to ride that monstrous wave), can help you find your balance. Remember, there's no shame in getting a surf instructor. Therapists are like the surf gurus of the habit world. They've got the skills, strategies, and they know how to ride the wave of change.

And remember, breaking a habit is more like surfing than walking. You have to ride the wave, not fight against it, and it's okay to wipe out every now and then (setbacks). Keep your eyes on the horizon, not on the reef beneath. Every attempt to stand up on the board, no matter how brief, is a victory, even if you tumble a bit, at least you're still in the water. After all, even the pros wipe out sometimes. It's called playing and having fun.

Habits manipulate their power in relationships, like that one friend who insists on always dominating the Apple remote. Positive rituals, like sharing finger foods and laughter, build trust, strengthen emotional bonds, and bring a relationship closer together. It's like having a personal comedy show on demand, complete with inside jokes and a laughter-filled love bonding.

On the flip side, negative habits are like a never-ending cycle of leaving dirty underwear on the floor or engaging in epic battles over who gets the last slice of pizza. They ignite recurring disputes, miscommunications, and create gaps between partners wider than the Grand Canyon. It's like being trapped in a bad comedy movie that never seems to find its punchline.

Imagine a partner who habitually forgets to put the cap back on the toothpaste, transforming the bathroom into a foamy mess every morning. It's funny but not funny, and a frustrating routine, where you can't help but chuckle at the absurdity of toothpaste wars before rushing off to work.

Or picture a partner with a tendency for spontaneous dance moves in the middle of serious conversations. While it adds a pocket-sized touch of hilarity, it typically leads to miscommunications and unmet needs getting lost in the rhythm of an unwanted TikTok.

The key is to recognize the impact of these habits and find a way to navigate them with a touch of humor and a mega dose of understanding. Perhaps you create a designated toothpaste cap holder or schedule occasional dance breaks to lighten the mood. Embracing the quirks and working together to establish positive habits can turn those comedic attempts into endearing moments that strengthen your bond.

So, let's rewrite the script, welcome some dumb humor, and remember that a little laughter can go a long way in navigating the ups and downs of habits within a relationship. After all, life is too short to miss out on the light-hearted side of a relationship.

Let's explore the importance of rituals and how to create better rituals to strengthen your relationship. Creating better rituals in marriage requires intention and commitment. Here are some tips to help you develop positive habits that will strengthen your relationship.

SET GOALS TOGETHER

Go to your favorite restaurant, coffee shop, or beach to discuss what you want to achieve in your marriage. This intentional and focused conversation can have a profound impact on strengthening your relationship. Here's a more detailed exploration of the process:

Choosing a comfortable and meaningful setting, such as your favorite restaurant, coffee shop, or beach, sets the stage for a relaxed and open conversation. It provides a backdrop that encourages connection and supports a deeper level of communication. Take it one step further and order for her but don't fuck it up.

Take the time to create an atmosphere of genuine curiosity and attentiveness. Encourage open dialogue by asking your partner lots of questions about their dreams, desires, and aspirations. Give them ample space to express themselves fully, and most importantly, truly listen to what they have to say. Active listening is key to understanding and connecting with your partner on a deeper level.

During this conversation, it's important to be truthful and express your own feelings and desires honestly. Share your thoughts, hopes, and concerns openly, creating an environment of vulnerability and authenticity. By expressing your true feelings, you create a safe space for your partner to do the same. Exemplifying your vulnerable side is key in this moment.

If you're concerned about remembering all the details, consider bringing a notepad to write down the key points of the conversation. I highly recommend you make notes. This helps ensure that nothing important gets missed or forgotten. By actively taking notes, you show your commitment to the process and signal that her words are valuable and will be remembered. To maintain focus and minimize distractions, it's best to leave your phone aside during this conversation. This shows respect and attentiveness towards your partner, demonstrating that they have your undivided attention.

Once you've identified your goals and dreams as a couple, it's important to break them down into simpler, achievable actions. This makes the goals more manageable and helps you track progress over time. Write down these action steps and consider posting them on your bathroom mirror or another visible place where you'll see them regularly. This serves as a reminder of your shared goals and reinforces your commitment to working on them together.

By reading these goals before bed and as the first thing in the morning, you set a positive and focused tone for your day. It helps you maintain a sense of purpose and reminds you of the actions you've committed to taking to strengthen your relationship.

Remember, the key to making this conversation successful is creating a safe, non-judgmental space where both partners feel heard and valued. Approach it with genuine curiosity, active listening, and an open heart. By dedicating time and effort to these intentional conversations, you lay a foundation for a stronger, more fulfilling marriage built on shared goals, effective communication, and mutual growth.

CONSISTENCY

Rituals are built through repetition and time, so consistency is key. It's important to make a plan and stick to it, even when it feels daunting. We all have days when we don't feel like putting in the effort, but staying committed to your chosen rituals is crucial for their effectiveness. This means no wavering or making excuses. Stay dedicated, even on those days when motivation is low.

One effective approach is to set aside specific times each week for activities that strengthen your bond. This could be a designated date night, morning surf, or a bike night, whatever activity works for you and her. By scheduling quality time together, you create a consistent habit of investing in your relationship.

During these dedicated times, make it a point to listen attentively when your wife speaks. Give her your full presence and focus. This means actively listening, paying attention to her words, and demonstrating empathy. It's also valuable to communicate openly and clarify how you can best support her. Asking a simple question like, "Do you want me to just listen or do you want help with a solution?" shows that you are attentive to her needs and willing to provide the support she desires. Asking the simple question of whether she wants you to solve or listen, works. As men, we are programmed to figure it out and women most times want you to listen. Ask her!

The ultimate goal is to nourish growth and support in your relationship through consistent rituals of working together. By establishing and maintaining these positive rituals, you create a foundation for mutual understanding, communication, and shared experiences. The key is to stay committed, adjust as needed, and embrace the journey of growth and connection with your wife.

Remember, forming consistent rituals requires effort and dedication, but the rewards are momentous. By prioritizing consistent quality time and active listening, you nurture a deeper bond and strengthen your relationship's foundation. So, make a plan, stick to it, and enjoy the journey of growth and connection as you build these positive rituals together.

ACCOUNTABLE

Creating positive rituals in a relationship is like becoming a superhero duo. You and your partner are on a mission to conquer those sneaky negative behaviors and save your relationship from averageville. But remember, even superheroes need accountability.

Imagine yourselves as the dynamic duo of "The Accountables." You wear matching capes, armed with truth and constructive feedback as your superpowers. Together, you're committed to calling out those negative behaviors faster than a speeding bullet and replacing them with rituals that make your relationship soar higher than a superhero in flight.

During your regular check-ins, use secret codenames like "Captain Communicator" and "Iron Feedback Master" to keep the mood light and playful. Share your progress with a victory dance or a celebratory high-five that would make even the Avengers proud.

And when it comes to offering constructive feedback, remember to use your superhero wit and charm. Sprinkle in some Iron Man-themed metaphors or puns to lighten the mood. Just be careful not to accidentally unleash your wife's secret power of eye-rolling.

Supporting each other's growth is like being sidekicks on an epic adventure. Together, you navigate the challenges and setbacks, complete with inside jokes and laughter. Let humor be the concrete that bonds you tighter than Spider-Man's webs, keeping your relationship enduring and lively.

In this super-heroic journey of accountability and positive habits, remember that even superheroes stumble and make mistakes. Embrace your uniqueness and laugh at the occasional slip-ups. With a shared sense of humor and the power of accountability, you'll navigate the challenges with a smile on your faces and your relationship will be stronger than a castle.

So, don your capes, embrace your inner Super Power, and get ready to save your relationship one ritual at a time. There's no challenge you can't conquer together.

SUCCESSES

When it comes to celebrating your successes, unleash your inner party animal. Break out the fire cannons, cue the strippers, and get ready to party like it's 1999. Who says positive rituals can't be celebrated with fire and strippers? Oh wait. That's pre-marriage. Yeah, don't do that.

Seriously, take a moment to raise your glasses and toast to your success. Feel free to keep it simple or make it an extravagant celebration. If you're in the mood for something more adventurous, how about planning a spontaneous vacation or a day filled with heart-pounding activities? Zip-lining through the trees or attempting a water sport to add an extra layer of amusement to the festivities.

Remember your inside jokes? Time to let them fly. Reminisce about those funny moments you shared during your journey of positive change. Laugh about that time you accidentally used salt instead of sugar while cooking together, turning your cookies into salt bombs. Embrace the humor in the small hiccups along the way, they make the celebration even more memorable.

So go ahead, celebrate your successes with a dash of humor, bottle of wine, and a whole lot of joy. Let your celebrations be as vibrant, silly, and unique as the two of you. After all, creating positive habits and strengthening your relationship should be a happy and laughter-filled adventure.

PATIENCE

In today's society of instant everything, patience can be as elusive as finding a parking spot at Costco. We live in a fast-paced society where we expect results faster than a motorcycle on the Salt Flats. But when it comes to building positive habits in marriage, patience becomes your dependable sidecar partner on the wild ride of marriage.

Creating rituals takes time, just like learning to ride a motorcycle without accidentally crashing into the neighbor's new Lamborghini. It's a journey filled with twists, turns, and occasional detours, much like ripping on a winding mountain road on two wheels. Fear not, fearless riders of the marriage highway, for every twist and turn brings you closer to mastering the art of positive rituals.

Patience might test your sanity, just like riding a motorcycle in a rainstorm without a windshield. You might feel like shouting, "What are we doing?" Remember, the journey is half the fun. Embrace the bumps in the road, the unexpected snowstorm, or the occasional gust of wind. Laugh at the absurdity of it all and keep the throttle twisted and let it be exhilarating.

Trust in the process, just like you trust your motorcycle to take you from point A to point B. Trust in the bond you've created. Rev up that engine of patience and hit the road with a sense of adventure. Embrace the unpredictable nature of building rituals, knowing that every twist and turn will lead you to a more fulfilling, peaceful, and loving relationship.

Remember to celebrate the small victories along the way. Imagine yourself cruising down the highway with your wife, wind blowing in your face and her hands wrapped around your waist. Raise your fist in the air and let out an elated "Fuck Yeah" . After all, what's a motorcycle ride without a little celebration at the end?

So, gear up, my patient riders of love. Embrace the winding road of building positive habits with a smile on your face and a mischievous twinkle in your eye. Embrace the unexpected detours, enjoy the exhilaration of the journey, and trust that your patience and commitment will lead you to the destination of a happy and fulfilling marriage. Let's hit the road, my two-wheeled warriors, and ride into the sunset of love, laughter, and adventure. And if you don't know how to ride a motorcycle, man-up motherfucker and learn how.

Positive rituals are like the secret sauce that adds spice and richness to our lives. When it comes to marriage, they become even more vital, serving as the foundation of a strong and thriving relationship. By consciously creating and cultivating positive habits, you lay the groundwork for a fulfilling and happy life together as a team.

Setting goals is like plotting the course of your journey. Just as a captain navigates a ship through rough waters, setting goals helps you and your wife chart a path towards an empowered and more loving relationship. Uncover the areas where you want to grow and improve, whether it's communication, quality time, or emotional intimacy. With defined goals in mind, you can steer your relationship towards greater happiness.

Consistency is the glue that holds your rituals together. It's the commitment to showing up and putting in the effort, day in and day out. Like a daily exercise routine that keeps you fit, consistent positive rituals in your marriage help build trust, strengthen emotional connections, and reinforce the bond between you and your wife or girlfriend.

Holding each other accountable is like having a cheerleader and a coach rolled into one. It's about being each other's support system, mildly nudging and reminding each other of the commitments you've made. By holding each other accountable, you create a sense of shared responsibility and motivate each other to stay on track.

Celebrating successes is the icing on the cake. It's the recognition and acknowledgment of the progress you've made together. When you achieve a goal or make positive strides in your relationship, take a moment to pause and celebrate. Whether it's a toast, a small gift, or a fun outing, celebrating successes strengthens your bond and reinforces the positive habits you've cultivated.

Patience is like a superpower that helps you weather the ups and downs of the journey. Life is a journey and building positive habits takes time. It's natural to encounter setbacks and challenges along the way. Patience allows you to approach these obstacles with a calm and understanding mindset, knowing that change and growth take time. It allows you to maintain focus on the progress you've made and remain committed to the long-term goals for your relationship.

By setting goals, being consistent, holding each other accountable, celebrating successes, and practicing patience, you lay the foundation for a stronger, more loving partnership. Positive habits become the fabric of your relationship, weaving together trust, respect, and emotional connection. They create a framework for a fulfilling and joyful life together.

So, embrace the power of rituals and set sail on the journey of creating a stronger and more loving partnership. With determination, mutual support, and a commitment to growth, you can cultivate the rituals that will transform your relationship into a flourishing and everlasting bond.

CONCLUSION

CONCLUSION

At the end of the day, relationships are less about finding perfection and more about learning, laughing, and loving through the imperfections. Whether you identify as the loyal Golden Retriever, anxious little Chihuahua, aloof Feral Cat, sly Fox, or wide-eyed Pomeranian, your attachment style is just one part of your love story, not the whole script.

The real win comes from self-awareness. When you recognize your patterns, you gain the power to shift them. When you understand your partner's language, whether that's through touch, time, words, gifts, or acts of service, you unlock new ways to connect. And when you both commit to building positive rituals, those small, consistent, sometimes silly but always meaningful rituals, you create a love that is resilient, playful, and deeply rooted.

Love, after all, is not a one-time grand gesture. It's in the little things: the goofy inside jokes, patience when the toothpaste cap is missing (again), forgiveness after a fight, the encouragement to grow, and the courage to stay. It's about riding the waves of attachment tendencies with humor, grace, and a willingness to keep showing up for each other.

So, as you walk away from these pages, remember this: you are not chained to the past, nor are you locked into one way of loving. You have the choice, every day, to practice secure, wholehearted love. And while it may not always look like a fairytale, it can absolutely feel like home.

Home is in the heart surrounded by love. Whatever your style, keep choosing love. Love is the greatest and most powerful emotion we can live from.

Because in the end, that's what makes the ride worth it. So, don't be a fucking idiot.

BIO

BIO

Blake is often seen as the quiet one in the room, but that quiet hides a mind that's always firing, bouncing from one idea to the next like sparks off a campfire. He's introspective, observant, and sharp, but his calm energy can shift into pure adventure when life calls for it. Ask him about his greatest accomplishment and you won't hear about work, travel, or success. Without hesitation, he'll tell you, it's being a dad.

Blake has two incredible kids who light up his world. He's spent countless hours traveling the globe with his son, chasing waves from California to Europe, Mexico, Indonesia, Japan, and Australia. They've surfed until sunset, camped in foreign lands, and built memories that live far beyond the shoreline. His daughter, strong, confident, and fiercely independent, dances through life with the same passion. They've enjoyed countless travel adventures as well. Watching her carve her own path fills him with pride and awe.

Before all that, Blake built a life in the movie business, a world of long days, bright lights, and creative chaos. He'd wake at 3 a.m., balancing life on set with his growing love for writing. While the rest of the world slept, he'd write screenplays, stories full of grit, humor, and heart. Over time, he penned ten screenplays and a children's book and a spiritual-adventure novel, each one a reflection of his wild imagination and relentless drive.

Adventure has always been stitched into his DNA. He's been riding motorcycles since he could walk, tearing across the Mojave Desert, sleeping beneath endless stars, and pushing through blizzards, tornadoes, and even across the Arctic Circle. Life hasn't just been about the smooth roads, it's been about the miles earned through courage and perseverance.

But even the strongest riders hit rough terrain. When Blake suffered a stroke, it was as if someone turned out the lights. The experience was humbling, terrifying, and transformative. It tested every ounce of his will and mental strength. Few knew what he was going through, but inside, he rebuilt himself to be stronger, steadier, more grateful. That moment reignited his passion for living.

Now, at 60, Blake's life is fuller and richer than ever. His mornings begin early with a good cup of coffee and quiet time with his two dogs and life partner. He surfs, lifts weights, hikes, swims, and feeds his mind the way he feeds his soul, with discipline, curiosity, and gratitude. He's in a great relationship, one that's grounded, loving, and real. The kind where laughter comes easy, respect runs deep, and both people bring out the best in each other.

Each day feels like another chance to live harder, love deeper, and paddle into life's next wave. And with every wave he catches, Blake strives to surf the next wave better. He's celebrating life. Blessed, grateful, and alive, he's exactly where he's meant to be.

www.ingramcontent.com/pod-product-compliance
Lightning Source LLC
Chambersburg PA
CBHW072100290426
44110CB00014B/1763